THE LITTLE PINK BOOK OF ROSÉ

the little Pink book of Rosé

Andrews McMeel
PUBLISHING®

introduction

A TOAST TO PINK

It's the wine of royals and aristocrats, movie stars and athletes. It's enjoyed in street-side cafés and trendy restaurants, at poolside barbecues and on tropical beaches. It's served at weddings in crystal flutes and at picnics in plastic cups. It's rosé—French for the word *pink*—and it's taking the wine world by storm.

The rosé revolution has actually been under way for the last several years. Why? First, it's one of the most versatile wines around. Not red, not white, but gloriously and unabashedly pink, rosé can be served on nearly any occasion and paired with a wide variety of foods. Looking for a wine to serve at the next book club meeting? A rich rosé from sunny California appeals to both red and white wine lovers. Wondering what to order with that spicy Indian curry? A nice crisp rosé from Provence will cool down the palate. Need a gift for your mother-in-law? A syrah-based rosé from Down Under is the ideal step up from her usual white zinfandel.

Second, rosé has been getting some serious love from winemakers around the world. Although once upon a time rosés were an underappreciated by-product of red-wine making, today many of these pink beauties are lovingly made using grapes and techniques normally reserved for higher-end wines. No

back in the day

In Greek and Roman times, all "red" wines were actually pink because the juice was always separated from the grape skins early in the wine-making process. This was probably to avoid spoilage—and so the wine would be ready to drink sooner!

longer an afterthought, rosés are gaining in
stature, becoming fixtures in fine restaurants,
garnering positive reviews from wine critics,
and occupying a place of honor on the tables
of wine drinkers everywhere. The world is
finally seeing through rosé-colored glasses!

ROSÉ IN A NUTSHELL

So what exactly is rosé? It is essentially a
broad category of wine, just as white wines
and red wines are. Indeed, it falls between the
two, at least colorwise. Most rosés are made
entirely from red grape varieties, though some
incorporate small amounts of white grapes
for different aromas and flavors. Any country
that grows red wine grapes can—and probably
does—produce rosé. You can find pink wines
from regions in France, Italy, Spain, California,

Australia, New Zealand, South Africa, and South America, and that's not even a complete list! And it should come as no surprise that the predominant red grape varieties in each region end up in those rosés. In the south of France, for example, popular red wine grapes such as grenache, mourvèdre, cinsault, syrah, and carignan often form the base of the area's rosés, and in Spain, you're likely to find tempranillo, garnacha, and graciano. In California, rosés are often made from zinfandel, pinot noir, syrah, or cabernet sauvignon.

STYLES & COLORS

With so many winemakers around the world producing rosés from different grape varieties and wine-making techniques, it's no wonder so many rosé styles exist. There are sweet rosés,

why it's pink

Like all red wines, the color of rosé is derived from the grape skins. But with rosé, the juice is separated from the skins (called *pressing* in wine lingo) much earlier in the wine-making process. Less skin contact equals less color, which is why rosés are pink instead of darker shades of red.

dry rosés, and rosés that are somewhere in the middle. And don't forget the sparkling rosés: Some of the most respected French Champagnes are made from red pinot noir or pinot meunier grapes. Sometimes called *blanc de noirs* (the term *Champagne* is reserved for wines from the Champagne region of France), these delightful pink sparklers are a category unto themselves.

And then there are the colors! From light salmon to bright watermelon to deep raspberry, the hues of rosé are as numerous as the colors of a sunset. And although it's risky to generalize with such a large category of wines, the color of a rosé can provide some indication of its origin and style. For instance, rosés that are darker and rosier are more likely to have come from warmer climates. They may also be more full bodied and have more berry-like flavors. Lighter-colored rosés, on the other hand, often come from cooler climates. They tend to be brighter and more crisp but still fruity, with flavors predominantly in the citrus range.

With so many rosés to choose from—and we seem to have more in restaurants and on store shelves every day—it's wise to ask your sommelier, server, or retailer for suggestions based on your taste preferences. Pay particular attention to dry versus sweet, as pink wines tend to come in a wider range of sweetness than traditional red and white wines.

ANY TIME CAN BE ROSÉ TIME

Nothing says summer like a perfectly chilled glass of rosé, especially when it's enjoyed outdoors in the company of good friends. Yet

Provence: rosé's home

Although rosé is produced in many parts of the world, the Côtes de Provence region in southern France is arguably its spiritual home. Rosé was brought to Provence by the Greeks in 600 BCE, and the area has specialized in the wine ever since. Today, strict rules govern allowable grape varieties and growing techniques to guarantee the quality of the region's rosés.

the versatility of rosé, and its many styles, means it can be savored year-round and at any occasion that calls for wine. In the south of France, particularly in Provence, which is arguably its birthplace, rosé can be found on café tables from morning until night, either as an ideal aperitif or as a harmonious accompaniment to the region's quintessential Mediterranean cuisine. In alpine lodges, rosés are a popular après-ski choice, well suited for warming the insides by a crackling fire. In many cities, rosé has even gained a following among men, spawning the term *brosé*. This normally pink-averse demographic has caught on to the pleasures of rosé, with some opting for a drink of pink over their usual artisanal brew.

DRINKING

TEMPERATURE

For the most pleasurable drinking experience,
rosé should be served cold, much like a white
wine, at 40° to 50°F. Sparkling and still rosés
on the sweet side should be served at the lower
end of that temperature range. Avoid allowing
the wine to get too cold, however, or its
delicate fruit flavors will be masked. To ensure
an appropriate temperature, place the bottle
in the refrigerator for an hour or two before
drinking. Alternatively, fill a bucket with equal
parts cold water and ice and immerse the
bottle in the bucket. The wine should be ready
to drink in about a half hour.

you say, I say

Rosé means *pink* in French, and in New World countries pink wines are generally also called *rosés* (or sometimes blush wines). In Spain, the term is *rosado*, and in Italy, it's *rosato*. In Germany, the wine is called *Weissherbst*.

AGING

Most rosés are made for early enjoyment and do not need to be cellared or aged. In general, rosés should be drunk within six months to a year of purchase. End of story.

GLASSWARE

It's been shown that proper glassware can enhance the experience of a wine, and for rosé, experts recommend a stemmed, tulip-shaped glass with a slightly tapered top (similar to most white wine glasses). Traditional champagne flutes are recommended for sparkling rosés, as they help to concentrate and preserve all those tiny bubbles.

HOWEVER, WHEN IN ROME . . .

Okay, okay, serving rosé at the proper temperature and in good glassware can enhance the experience of the wine. But the beauty of rosé is that it's one of the most casual quaffs around. So go ahead and take it to the beach in a thermos, pour it over ice at a picnic, sip it out of a plastic tumbler at the movies. The point is, enjoy it. Don't overthink the pink!

FOOD LOVES ROSÉ

Rosés are some of the world's most food-friendly wines, especially those that display a careful balance of fruit and acidity. Of course, the type of rosé you choose will depend on your personal preference. Do you like sweet, dry, or somewhere in between? Do you favor full-bodied and generous or fresh, light, and crisp?

In general, the most important element to keep in mind when pairing rosé with food

rosé goes Hollywood

Rosé had a star turn in the movie *An Affair to Remember* when Cary Grant and Deborah Kerr discovered their mutual affection for pink Champagne (and then each other). Rosé has also captured the hearts of recent Hollywood players, including Francis Ford Coppola, whose California winery produces Sofia rosé, named after his daughter.

is the sweetness of the wine. Rosés that are slightly sweet (off dry) are well suited to casual fare (think beach outings and picnics) and to fragrant, highly spiced dishes (think Indian curries, *biryani*, and tandoori; Thai curries and spicy salads; Vietnamese *pho* and noodle dishes). They can also be suitably paired with some desserts, as long as they're not too sweet.

Dry rosés, which tend to be lighter and more crisp, pair well with such classic Mediterranean dishes as ratatouille, bouillabaisse, and *moules à la marinière*. But they can also be successfully paired with nearly any food you would serve with a dry white wine or even a light-bodied red, such as pinot noir. Go ahead and try them with savory appetizers and main courses, but keep in mind that dry rosés, like most dry wines, are not a great match for sweet foods.

Sparkling rosés tend to be on the drier side and are fantastic with any foods you would normally pair with sparkling wine or Champagne. Oysters on the half shell, smoked salmon, deviled eggs, and even heartier dishes, such as risotto, roast chicken, or pork roast, arc immediately elevated to a celebration when enjoyed with a sparkling rosé.

I believe in pink.

—AUDREY HEPBURN

A MEAL WITHOUT WINE IS LIKE A DAY WITHOUT SUNSHINE.

—JEAN ANTHELME BRILLAT-SAVARIN

ALWAYS CARRY A corkscrew AND THE WINE SHALL PROVIDE ITSELF.

—BASIL BUNTING

*Where there is no wine,
there is no love.*

—EURIPIDES

It's a smile.
It's a kiss.
It's a sip of wine.
It's summertime!

—KENNY CHESNEY

Rosé is a wine
that entertains
long before
it even passes
your lips.

—MARK OLDMAN

A GOOD ROSÉ ... IS A WINE WHERE ONCE YOU HAVE A GLASS YOU SAY TO YOURSELF "WHY NOT ANOTHER?"

—ALAIN COMBARD, VINTNER

It's approachable but not cloying; it's fragrant and pretty and refreshing and easy to drink.

—CHARLES PERRY, *LOS ANGELES TIMES*

A glass of wine in one's hand is rather like a jewel, isn't it, a large, liquid one?

—MARIE RUTKOSKI

THE WORLD LOOKS BETTER THROUGH ROSÉ-COLORED GLASSES.

It warms the blood,
adds luster to the eyes,
and wine and love have
ever been allies.

—OVID

ROSÉ
MAKES THE
FUTURE
LOOK
ROSY!

Fan the sinking flame of hilarity with the wing of friendship; and pass the rosy wine.

—CHARLES DICKENS

ROSÉ
IS A
sunset
IN A
GLASS.

The flavor of wine is like delicate poetry.

—LOUIS PASTEUR

Wine makes
every meal
an occasion,
every table
more elegant,
every day
more civilized.

– ANDRÉ SIMON

IN THE ABSTRACT
ART OF COOKING . . .
WINE MAKES
EVEN THE WORST
CULINARY DISASTER
TASTE DELICIOUS.

—BOB BLUMER

ROSÉ IS LIKE KETCHUP:

it goes with everything.

A meal without rosé is called breakfast.

I never taste
the wine first
in restaurants,
I just ask the
waiter to pour.

—NIGELLA LAWSON

WHAT CONTEMPTIBLE SCOUNDREL STOLE THE CORK FROM MY LUNCH?

—W. C. FIELDS

MONDAY. . . .

Nothing a glass of rosé can't fix.

T.G.I.F̶.R.—
Thank God It's Rosé-day!

I NEED COFFEE TO HELP ME CHANGE THE THINGS I CAN

. . . AND WINE TO HELP ME ACCEPT THE THINGS I CAN'T!

—TANYA MASSE

SEIZE THE DAY THEN SIP ROSÉ.

A DRINK A DAY

keeps the shrink away.

—EDWARD ABBEY

WINE
IS AT THE
HEAD OF ALL
MEDICINES;
WHERE WINE
IS LACKING,
DRUGS
ARE NECESSARY.

—BABYLONIAN TALMUD: BABA BATHRA

PINK IS THE NEW NAVY.

—DIANA VREELAND

Rosé...
is the little
black dress
of pink wines.

—WINE FOLLY

THE COLOR
PINK
MAKES EVERYTHING LOOK PRETTY.

There's something kind of decadent about drinking rosé.

—SAM DALY, ACTOR

PINK ISN'T JUST A COLOR, IT'S AN ATTITUDE!

—MILEY CYRUS

RAISE YOUR GLASS IF YOU ARE WRONG IN ALL THE RIGHT WAYS!

—PINK, SONGWRITER

PINK WINE MAKES ME SLUTTY.

—ZOOEY DESCHANEL, ON *NEW GIRL*

You can
learn a lot
about a
woman
by getting
smashed
with her.

—TOM WAITS

ROSÉ:

young, cheap, and ideal for mixing.

REAL MEN DRINK PINK.

—THOMAS PASTUSZAK, WINE DIRECTOR

YES, YOU CAN DRINK ROSÉ AND STILL BE A BADASS.

—CHARLES & CHARLES

Men are like a fine wine. They all start out like grapes, and it's our job to stomp on them and keep them in the dark until they mature into something you'd like to have dinner with.

—JILL SHALVIS

WINE
IS TO WOMEN
AS
DUCT TAPE
IS TO MEN.

It fixes everything.

—TANYA MASSE

WHO DOES NOT LOVE WINE, WOMEN, AND SONG REMAINS A FOOL HIS WHOLE LIFE LONG.

—MARTIN LUTHER

God made only water, but man made wine.

—VICTOR HUGO

WINE AND FRIENDS ARE A GREAT BLEND.

—ERNEST HEMINGWAY

WATER
SEPARATES THE PEOPLE OF THE WORLD;
WINE
UNITES THEM.

THE BEST WINE PAIRING IS WINE AND GOOD FRIENDS.

A bottle of wine begs to be shared; I have never met a miserly wine lover.

—CLIFTON FADIMAN

FRIENDS
DON'T LET
FRIENDS
DRINK ROSÉ
ALONE.

WINE
IS JUST A
CONVERSATION
WAITING TO
HAPPEN.

—JESSICA ALTIERI

FROM WINE WHAT SUDDEN FRIENDSHIP SPRINGS.

—JOHN GAY

Accept what life
offers you and try
to drink from
every cup. All wines
should be tasted;
some should only
be sipped, but others,
drink the whole bottle.

—PAULO COELHO

WHEN LIFE GIVES YOU LEMONS, SELL THEM TO BUY ROSÉ.

WINE

makes all things possible.

—GEORGE R. R. MARTIN

Wine makes daily living easier, less hurried, with fewer tensions and more tolerance.

—BENJAMIN FRANKLIN

ROSÉ THE DAY AWAY.

Wine cheers the sad,
revives the old,
inspires the young,
makes weariness forget
his toil.

—LORD BYRON

SAVE WATER, DRINK ROSÉ.

In water one sees one's own face;
but in wine, one beholds the
heart of another.

— FRENCH PROVERB

La vie en rosé:

Life through rosé-colored glasses.

Always

LOOK ON
THE ROSÉ SIDE
OF LIFE.

Wine is sunlight, held together by water.

—GALILEO GALILEI

IT DOESN'T
MATTER IF
THE GLASS
IS HALF EMPTY
OR HALF
FULL; THERE
IS CLEARLY
ROOM FOR
MORE WINE.

WINE IS A BRIDE WHO BRINGS A GREAT DOWRY TO THE MAN WHO WOOS HER PERSISTENTLY AND GRACEFULLY.

—EVELYN WAUGH

DOMESTIC BLISS:

Only a bottle of rosé away!

WINE IS ONE OF THE MOST CIVILIZED THINGS IN THE WORLD.

—ERNEST HEMINGWAY

Great wine requires a madman to grow the vine, a wise man to watch over it, a lucid poet to make it, and a lover to drink it.

—SALVADOR DALI

BE CAREFUL TO TRUST A PERSON WHO DOES NOT LIKE WINE.

—KARL MARX

I shall drink
no wine before
its time!
OK, it's time.

—GROUCHO MARX

The discovery of
a good wine is
increasingly better
for mankind than
the discovery of
a new star.

—LEONARDO DA VINCI

WINE IS BOTTLED POETRY.

—ROBERT LOUIS STEVENSON

NO·ROSÉ·PHOBIA:

The fear of running out of rosé.

KEEP
CALM
AND
DRINK
ROSÉ.

ROSÉ:
Summer Water.

—ERICA BLUMENTHAL AND NIKKI HUGANIR,
YES WAY ROSÉ

A rosé enthusiast:

Someone who becomes more enthusiastic
the more she drinks rosé.

IF REASSURANCES COULD DULL PAIN, NOBODY WOULD EVER GO TO THE TROUBLE OF PRESSING GRAPES.

—SCOTT LYNCH

Good wine
is a good familiar
creature,
if it be well used.

—WILLIAM SHAKESPEARE

ONE OF THE
DISADVANTAGES
OF WINE, IT
MAKES A MAN
MISTAKE WORDS
FOR THOUGHTS.

—SAMUEL JOHNSON

HERE'S TO ALCOHOL, THE ROSE-COLORED GLASSES OF LIFE.

—F. SCOTT FITZGERALD

TRUTH COMES OUT IN WINE.

—PLINY THE ELDER

The happiest
people don't
have the best of
everything...
they just
drink wine.

—TANYA MASSE

The wine—it made her limbs
loose and liquid, made her feel
that a hummingbird had taken
the place of her heart.

—JODI PICOULT

Rosé is the color
of perfection.~

WE ARE ALL MORTAL UNTIL THE FIRST KISS AND THE SECOND GLASS OF WINE.

--EDUARDO GALEANO

Clearly, the pleasures wines afford are transitory—but so are those of the ballet, or of a musical performance. Wine is inspiring and adds greatly to the joy of living.

—NAPOLEON

AGE GETS BETTER WITH WINE.

What though youth
gave love and roses,
Age still leaves us
friends and wine.

—THOMAS MOORE

GIVE ME ROSÉ OVER ROSES ANY DAY.

Wine improves with age.
I like it more the older I get.

There is a communion of more than our bodies when bread is broken and wine drunk.

—M. F. K. FISHER

A WALTZ AND A GLASS OF WINE INVITE AN ENCORE.

—JOHANN STRAUSS

JUST THE SIMPLE ACT OF TASTING A GLASS OF WINE IS ITS OWN EVENT.

—DAVID HYDE PIERCE

I cook
with wine.

Sometimes
I even add it
to the food.

—W. C. FIELDS

A MAN WILL BE ELOQUENT IF YOU GIVE HIM GOOD WINE.

—RALPH WALDO EMERSON

Wine can of their
wits the wise beguile,
Make the sage folic,
and the serious smile.

—HOMER

Within the bottle's depths, the wine's soul sang one night.

—CHARLES BAUDELAIRE

ROSES ARE PINK,
SO IS MY WINE.
REFILL MY GLASS,
AND I'LL BE
JUST FINE.

What is better than to
sit at the table at the end
of the day and drink
wine with friends, or
substitutes for friends?

—JAMES JOYCE

An empty rosé bottle is filled with happy memories.

Give me wine to wash me clean of the weather-stains of cares.

—RALPH WALDO EMERSON

LET US HAVE
WINE AND
WOMEN, MIRTH
AND LAUGHTER,
SERMONS AND
SODA WATER
THE DAY AFTER.

—LORD BYRON

ANYTHING
is possible
with
SUNSHINE
and a little
PINK.

—LILLY PULITZER

bites

OYSTERS ON THE HALF SHELL WITH SPARKLING ROSÉ MIGNONETTE

makes 12 oysters; serves 2 to 4

MIGNONETTE

2 tablespoons champagne vinegar

2 tablespoons finely chopped shallot

⅛ teaspoon sea salt

Pinch of black pepper

2 tablespoons brut sparkling rosé, chilled

Crushed ice, for serving

12 oysters, shucked

1. To make the mignonette, combine the vinegar, shallot, salt, and pepper in a small bowl, stir well, and let stand for 15 minutes. Just before serving, stir in the rosé.

2. Line a platter or tray with ice. Arrange the oysters on the ice and spoon about 1 teaspoon mignonette over each oyster. Serve immediately.

ONE-BITE PEACH, MOZZARELLA, AND BASIL SKEWERS WITH ROSÉ-BALSAMIC SYRUP

makes 24 skewers

½ cup crisp, fruity rosé, such as pinot noir

½ cup white balsamic vinegar

2 teaspoons sugar

2 large, ripe but firm yellow peaches

24 medium-size fresh basil leaves

24 mozzarella ciliegine (cherry-size balls), drained (8 to 10 ounces)

Salt and freshly ground black pepper

1. Combine the rosé, vinegar, and sugar in a small saucepan and bring to a boil over medium-high heat. Boil for about 8 minutes, or until reduced by about two-thirds. Remove from the heat and let cool to room temperature.

2. Have ready 24 toothpicks. Halve and pit each peach. Cut each half into 3 wedges, then halve each wedge crosswise. Spear 1 peach chunk, 1 basil leaf, and 1 mozzarella ball onto each toothpick and arrange the skewers on a platter. Drizzle the cooled syrup over the skewers and season lightly with salt and pepper. Serve immediately.

ROSÉ QUICK PICKLES

makes 2 quarts

2 pounds assorted vegetables (such as cauliflower, radishes, baby carrots, and fennel bulbs)

8 dill sprigs

BRINE

2 cups water

1 cup Provençal rosé

1 cup white wine vinegar

½ cup sugar

¼ cup kosher salt

2 bay leaves

1 teaspoon black peppercorns

1 teaspoon coriander seeds

1 teaspoon yellow mustard seeds

SPECIAL EQUIPMENT

2 (1-quart) mason jars

1. Trim the vegetables as needed. Divide the cauliflower into florets, slice the fennel, and leave the radishes and carrots whole. Tightly pack the vegetables into the jars. Place 4 dill sprigs in each jar.

2. To make the brine, combine all of the ingredients in a medium saucepan and bring to a boil over high heat, stirring until the sugar and salt dissolve. Pour the hot brine over the vegetables, immersing them. Seal each jar with its lid and let cool to room temperature, then refrigerate for at least 24 hours before serving. The pickles will keep for up to 2 weeks.

ROSÉ-AND-CHILE-POACHED SHRIMP WITH AVOCADO CREAM

serves 4 to 6

SHRIMP

2 cups Provençal rosé

2 cups water

Juice of ½ lemon

1 jalapeño chile, stemmed and sliced crosswise

2 teaspoons salt

1 pound extra-large shrimp (18/20 count), peeled and deveined, with tails intact

AVOCADO CREAM

2 ripe avocados, halved, pitted, and peeled

1 tablespoon sour cream

2 teaspoons fresh lime juice

¼ teaspoon salt

Dash of hot sauce, such as Tabasco

1. To cook the shrimp, have ready a bowl of ice water. Combine the rosé, water, lemon juice, jalapeño, and salt in a medium saucepan and bring to a boil over high heat. Decrease the heat to low, add the shrimp, and poach for about 3 minutes, or until cooked through. Drain and immediately immerse in the ice water to stop the cooking. Drain again, cover, and chill while you prepare the sauce.

2. To make the avocado cream, combine all of the ingredients in a food processor and process until light and smooth. Season to taste, then transfer to a serving bowl.

3. Arrange the shrimp on a serving platter and serve with the avocado cream for dipping.

PINK GAZPACHO SHOOTERS WITH SLIVERED ALMONDS AND GRAPES

makes about 2 cups; serves 6 to 8

2 slices country-style white bread, lightly toasted, crusts removed, and cut into cubes (about 2 cups)

2 cups ice water, divided

1 cup blanched whole almonds, lightly toasted

2 cloves garlic, chopped

½ cup white grape juice

¼ cup fruity Spanish rosado, chilled

¼ cup extra-virgin olive oil

1 tablespoon sherry vinegar

½ teaspoon salt

¼ teaspoon black pepper

Slivered almonds, lightly toasted, for garnish

Seedless green grapes, sliced, for garnish

1. Place the bread in a medium bowl, add 1 cup of the ice water, and let soak for 1 minute. Remove the bread and squeeze out any excess water.

2. Combine the whole almonds and garlic in a food processor and process until finely chopped. Add the soaked bread, the remaining 1 cup ice water, grape juice, *rosado*, and oil and process until smooth, about 2 minutes. Add the vinegar, salt, and pepper and pulse to combine. Pour the mixture through a fine-mesh sieve set over a medium bowl, pressing on the solids with the back of a spoon to extract as much liquid as possible. Discard the solids. Cover the liquid and refrigerate for at least 2 hours or up to 8 hours.

3. To serve, pour the gazpacho into 6 to 8 shooter glasses, depending on size. Garnish with the slivered almonds and grapes.

cocktails

ROSÉ LEMONADE

serves 8

3½ cups water, divided
½ cup sugar
1 cup fresh lemon juice
1 lemon, thinly sliced crosswise
1 (750-ml) bottle Provençal rosé, chilled
Ice cubes, for serving

1. Combine ½ cup of the water and the sugar in a small saucepan and bring to a boil over medium heat, stirring to dissolve the sugar. Remove the syrup from the heat and let cool to room temperature.

2. Combine the cooled syrup, the remaining 3 cups water, the lemon juice, and the lemon slices in a large pitcher, stir well, and refrigerate until chilled.

3. Just before serving, fill 8 glasses with ice. Add the rosé to the pitcher, stir well, and pour into the glasses.

SPARKLING ROSÉ
APEROL SPRITZ

serves 1

Ice cubes, for serving
1½ ounces Aperol (Italian bitter orange liqueur)
3 ounces demi-sec sparkling rosé (such as rosé moscato
    or spumante), chilled
Splash of sparkling water or club soda
1 orange slice, for garnish

Chill a large wineglass. Fill the glass with ice and add the
Aperol and rosé. Top with the sparkling water and stir well.
Garnish with the orange slice.

PINK SANGRIA

serves 8

1 orange, halved lengthwise, thinly sliced crosswise, and seeded
1 yellow peach, halved, pitted, and thinly sliced
½ lemon, halved lengthwise, thinly sliced crosswise, and seeded
1 cup raspberries
1 (750-ml) bottle fruity Spanish rosado, chilled
½ cup fresh orange juice
¼ cup orange liqueur, such as Cointreau
1 (750-ml) bottle demi-sec sparkling rosé, such as Spanish cava, chilled

1. Combine the orange, peach, lemon, and raspberries in a large pitcher. Add the *rosado*, orange juice, and orange liqueur, stir well, and refrigerate for 1 hour.

2. Just before serving, add the sparkling rosé and stir well.

KIR BLUSH ROYALE

serves 1

1 ounce crème de cassis
5 ounces brut sparkling rosé, chilled

Chill a champagne flute. Pour the crème de cassis into the flute, then slowly pour in the rosé.

SPARKLING ROSÉ BELLINI

serves 6

3 ripe white peaches, halved, pitted, peeled, and
    chopped
1 tablespoon fresh lemon juice
1 tablespoon sugar
1 (750-ml) bottle pinot noir sparkling rosé, such as
    Crémant d'Alsace brut rosé, chilled
Raspberry liqueur, such as framboise, for serving
    (optional)

1. Combine the peaches, lemon juice, and sugar in a food
processor and process until smooth. Transfer the purée to
a small bowl, cover, and refrigerate for about 1 hour, or
until cold.

2. Spoon about 1½ ounces peach purée into each of
6 champagne flutes. Divide the rosé evenly among the
glasses. Top each glass with a splash of the liqueur, if using.

BLACKBERRY ROSÉ MOJITO

serves 1

3 fresh mint leaves, plus 1 leaf for garnish
¼ cup blackberries, plus 1 berry for garnish
1 tablespoon sugar or agave syrup
½ lime, quartered
1½ ounces white rum
Crushed ice, for mixing and serving
3 ounces dry, fruity sparkling rosé, chilled

1. Chill a cocktail glass. Place the mint, blackberries, sugar, and lime in a cocktail shaker. Using a muddler or the back of a wooden spoon, muddle the ingredients together. Add the rum, fill the shaker with ice, cover, and shake until well chilled.

2. Fill the glass with ice and strain the contents of the shaker into the glass. Pour in the rosé and garnish with the mint leaf and blackberry.

RASPBERRY ROSÉ LIMONCELLO COCKTAIL

serves 1

¼ cup raspberries, plus 1 berry for garnish
¼ lemon, cut into 3 or 4 wedges
1 tablespoon sugar
1 ounce limoncello
¾ ounce vodka
Crushed ice, for mixing and serving
3 ounces dry, fruity sparkling rosé, chilled
Lemon peel twist, for garnish

1. Chill a cocktail glass. Place the raspberries, lemon wedges, sugar, and limoncello in a cocktail shaker. Using a muddler or the back of a wooden spoon, muddle the ingredients together. Add the vodka, fill the shaker with ice, cover, and shake until well chilled.

2. Fill the glass with ice and strain the contents of the shaker into the glass. Pour in the rosé and garnish with the raspberry and lemon peel.

ROSÉ GRAPEFRUIT VODKA COOLER

serves 1

Ice cubes, for mixing and serving
3 ounces crisp, fruity rosé (such as pinot noir or
    mourvèdre)
1½ ounces pink grapefruit vodka
½ ounce fresh lemon juice
½ ounce grenadine
Sparkling rosé or sparkling water, for topping off

1. Chill a rocks glass. Fill a cocktail shaker with ice cubes.
Add the rosé, vodka, lemon juice, and grenadine, cover,
and shake until well chilled.

2. Fill the glass with ice and strain the contents of the
shaker into the glass. Top with the sparkling rosé.

ROSÉRITA

serves 1

Ice cubes, for mixing
3 ounces crisp, fruity rosé (such as pinot noir or
    mourvèdre)
1 ounce silver tequila
½ ounce triple sec
½ ounce agave syrup
½ ounce fresh lime juice
1 thin lime slice, for garnish

1. Chill a cocktail glass. Fill a cocktail shaker with ice
cubes, add the rosé, tequila, triple sec, agave syrup, and
lime juice, cover, and shake until well chilled.

2. Strain the contents of the shaker into the glass. Garnish
with the lime slice and serve immediately.

FROSÉ STRAWBERRY DAIQUIRI

serves 6

1 (750-ml) bottle dry, fruity rosé (such as pinot noir
   or Provençal)
1 pound strawberries, hulled and coarsely chopped
¼ cup sugar
¼ cup white rum
¼ cup fresh lime juice
6 thin lime slices, for garnish

1. Pour the rosé into a freezer-proof pan and freeze until
mostly solid, at least 6 hours. (It will not freeze solidly
because of the alcohol.) Chill 6 cocktail glasses.

2. Place the strawberries in a medium bowl, sprinkle the
sugar on top, and lightly mash with a fork until the sugar
dissolves. Let stand for 10 minutes to macerate.

3. Transfer the strawberries to a food processor or blender,
add the rum and lime juice, and process until smooth. Add
the frozen rosé and pulse until slushy. Divide evenly among
the glasses and garnish each glass with a lime slice.

desserts

ROSÉ-AND-ORANGE-POACHED PEARS

serves 4

1 (750-ml) bottle cabernet sauvignon rosé

¾ cup sugar

2 tablespoons orange liqueur, such as Cointreau

Peel of ½ orange

Peel of ½ lemon

1 tablespoon peeled, coarsely grated fresh ginger

½ teaspoon ground cardamom

4 firm, but ripe Bosc or Bartlett pears, peeled, with
    stems intact

1 tablespoon finely grated orange zest, for garnish

1. Combine the rosé, sugar, liqueur, citrus peels, ginger, and cardamom in a medium saucepan and bring to a simmer over medium heat, stirring to dissolve the sugar.

2. Add the pears and immerse them in the liquid, adding water if needed to cover. Decrease the heat to medium-low, cover partially, and poach for about 20 minutes, or until the pears are tender but not mushy when pierced with a knife tip. Using a slotted spoon, transfer the pears to a large plate.

3. Bring the cooking liquid to a boil over high heat and boil for 15 to 20 minutes, until the liquid is reduced by about one-third. Remove from the heat and strain through a fine-mesh sieve placed over a medium bowl. Let cool to slightly warm or room temperature.

4. To serve, place each pear in a shallow serving bowl, spoon the syrup over the pears, and garnish with the orange zest.

ROSÉ GELÉE WITH RASPBERRIES, BLUEBERRIES, AND POMEGRANATE

serves 6

1 (¼-ounce) envelope unflavored powdered gelatin
1 cup water, divided
⅓ cup sugar
2 cups demi-sec sparkling rosé, such as pink moscato
1 cup raspberries
½ cup blueberries
1 tablespoon pomegranate seeds

1. In a medium heatproof bowl, sprinkle the gelatin over ½ cup of the water and let stand for 5 minutes, or until softened.

2. Combine the sugar and the remaining ½ cup water in a small saucepan and bring to a simmer over medium heat, stirring until the sugar dissolves. Remove the syrup from the heat, add it to the gelatin, and stir until the gelatin dissolves. Stir in the rosé and let stand until the foam subsides.

3. Divide the raspberries, blueberries, and pomegranate arils evenly among 6 wineglasses. Pour the rosé mixture over the fruit, dividing it evenly. Cover each glass with plastic wrap and refrigerate for at least 12 hours or up to overnight before serving.

SUMMER FRUIT SOUP WITH WHIPPED MASCARPONE CREAM

serves 6

1¼ cups fruity rosé (such as California pinot noir or
   Loire Rosé d'Anjou)
½ cup sugar
¼ cup fresh lemon juice
1 teaspoon finely grated orange zest
3 plums, halved, pitted, and each half cut into 3 wedges
2 peaches, halved, pitted, and each half cut into
   4 wedges
½ cup seedless red grapes
1 cup blackberries

MASCARPONE CREAM

4 ounces mascarpone cheese, at room temperature
½ cup heavy cream
2 tablespoons sugar
1 teaspoon fresh lemon juice

1. Combine the rosé, sugar, lemon juice, and orange zest in a medium saucepan and bring to a boil over medium-high heat, stirring until the sugar dissolves. Add the plums and peaches, decrease the heat to medium, and simmer for 3 minutes. Add the grapes and simmer for 1 minute. Stir in the blackberries, remove from the heat, and let stand for 15 minutes.

2. Transfer the fruit and liquid to a medium bowl, cover, and refrigerate for at least 2 hours, until cold, or up to 8 hours.

3. To make the mascarpone cream, place the mascarpone, cream, sugar, and lemon juice in a small bowl and whisk until soft peaks form.

4. To serve, ladle the fruit and its juices into 6 serving glasses or bowls and top each bowl with a dollop of the cream.

ROSÉ GRANITA WITH LEMON AND STRAWBERRY SYRUP

makes about 1½ quarts

12 ounces strawberries, hulled and chopped

½ cup water

½ cup sugar

1 tablespoon fresh lemon juice

1 (750-ml) bottle crisp, fruity rosé (such as pinot noir or mourvèdre)

1. Combine the strawberries, water, sugar, and lemon juice in a medium saucepan and bring to a boil over medium heat. Boil for about 2 minutes, then remove from the heat and let cool to room temperature.

2. Transfer the cooled strawberry syrup to a blender or food processor and process until smooth. Add the rosé and process until blended.

3. Pour the mixture into a shallow, freezer-proof metal baking pan or cake pan. Freeze for 1 hour, then scrape the partially frozen mixture thoroughly with a fork, separating it into crystals. Return the mixture to the freezer and continue to freeze for at least 8 hours, scraping again about every 3 to 4 hours to loosen the crystals.

4. To serve, fluff the crystals with a fork and then scoop into small bowls. Store in an airtight container in the freezer for up to 1 week.

ROSÉ-SPIKED WATERMELON BALLS WITH LIME AND MINT

serves 6 to 8

1 small seedless watermelon, halved and flesh scooped
   with a melon baller (about 6 cups)
½ cup crisp, fruity rosé (such as pinot noir or
   mourvèdre)
¼ cup fresh lime juice
2 tablespoons chopped fresh mint

1. Combine the watermelon, rosé, and lime juice in a large bowl and stir gently to mix well. Cover and refrigerate for at least 1 hour or up to overnight, stirring occasionally.

2. Spoon the watermelon balls into a serving bowl, garnish with the mint, and serve chilled with toothpicks for spearing.

Andrews McMeel Publishing
a division of Andrews McMeel Universal
1130 Walnut Street, Kansas City, Missouri 64106

www.andrewsmcmeel.com

17 18 19 20 21 TEN 10 9 8 7 6 5 4 3 2 1

ISBN: 978-1-4494-8699-0

Library of Congress Control Number: 2016960061

Editor: Allison Adler
Art Director: Holly Swayne
Production Editor: Erika Kuster
Production Manager: Tamara Haus

Attention: Schools and Businesses
Andrews McMeel books are available at quantity discounts
with bulk purchase for educational, business, or sales
promotional use. For information, please e-mail the
Andrews McMeel Publishing Special Sales Department:
specialsales@amuniversal.com.